GWYDION'S PLAN'
THE DEFINI'
MOON-PLANTING

C000285854

A Framework for all Years.

Half-monthly lists of virtually every vegetable suitable for sowing/planting during the month concerned, and monthly headings with write-in boxes to plan 'time-slots'. A brief introduction and key explain the steps involved.

The Primary Moon-planting Technique.

Understanding and identifying Moon phase time-slots, and how to apply them. A fascinating method to determine the Moon's phase at any time is included, so you may apply the Primary technique with only this Guide, every year.

The Secondary Moon-planting Technique.

Understanding and identifying 'Moon in Zodiac' time-slots, and how to apply them. What is the Zodiac, and why does the Moon's passage through it affect your gardening?

More Natural Techniques.

Other 'cyclic' considerations and how to designate all other plants for Moon-planting; flowers, major cereal crops, etc: (page 22) Companion and incompatible crops: (p. 24) Organic remedies for pests and diseases: (p. 26) Crop rotation, tips on composting: (p. 30) Daylight Saving Time adjustment, Planting Guide Year Sheets: (p. 32 & endpage)

From the **PAN-DIMENSIONAL** © Collection

Written, typeset and published by J. R. Gower, 1994.

*11, Summerhouse Orchard Cottages, Bove Town,
Glastonbury, Somerset. BA6 8JA*

ISBN 0 9523424 0 5

Printed at Walton Press, Glastonbury, Somerset, Great Britain.

INTRODUCTION

You may simply wish to use the listings without confining your sowing and planting within selected periods (time-slots) for Moon planting. Nonetheless, always check the suppliers' directions as new varieties are often available which may be sown earlier or later. If you live in particularly warm or cool/northern areas, you may sow many crops a couple of weeks earlier or later respectively - if unsure, ask local gardeners. The 'Plant out from greenhouse or frame' lists may also be varied according to weather and growth.

The Moon-planting time-slots: Turn back to the inside front cover, and read 'HOW TO USE THIS GUIDE' thoroughly. Now read through the following steps once (they refer to the similarly numbered parts of the key), then turn to Sections Two (pages 16-19) and Three (pages 20-21). Read these, then complete the steps for the monthly headings referring to Sections Two & Three as necessary.

Part [1.] Write in the dates, and if possible times, of New and Full Moons in the boxes provided. Section Two includes, if necessary, directions for identifying the Moon's phases whenever the Moon is visible.

Part [2.] The 'Primary' Technique: Transfer the Full & New Moon dates to the boxes provided, deducting 2 or 3 days from each as appropriate. (Follow the procedure given in Section Two, page 17.) These dates define the month's 'Moon phase time-slots'. You may use just these for sowing, etc., or complete the next step.

Part [3.] The 'Secondary' Technique: Read Section Three (pages 20-21) before copying the month's Moon/Zodiac Sign entry times into the paired boxes provided. Be sure to start with an appropriate 'beneficial Sign' as explained. Each pair of boxes represents the duration of a 'Zodiacal time-slot'. With these completed you may indicate, as illustrated, the longer 'Moon phase time-slots' above the Zodiac slots.

KEY: Sections Two & Three give detailed directions. Example: *(for January in the year of publication)* Looking at the January lists, I may sow tomatoes (last half of month, heated frame etc., no asterisk ✱, so 'All others' category) within the 'All others' Moon phase slot, and for the 'secondary' technique, in suitable 'Zodiac' slots: 14th (22.04 hrs.) to 17th (8.42hrs.) and 19th-22nd at the times shown. (10th-12th Jan. is probably too early.)

[1.] Full & New Moons

FULL	NEW	FULL	NEW
DATE	DATE *11th*	DATE *27th*	DATE
TIME	TIME *23.10*	TIME *13.23*	TIME

January

REFER TO KEY ON PAGE 2.

[2.] 'Moon phase' slots

	FROM DATE	TO DATE	FROM DATE	TO DATE
✱ Root veg: 2 days before Full to 3 days before New.	*from start*	*8th*	*25th*	*to end*
All others: 2 days before New to 3 days before Full.	*9th*	*24th*		

[3.] Slots when Moon is in Zodiacal signs: ♉ ♋ ♍ ♏ ♑ ♓ To complete, read key (page 2) & Sect. 3.(p.20)

←Root veg.— 8th/23.10↓ ↓9th —All others— 24th/13.23↓ ↓25th—Root veg.→

SIGN	♍	♎	♏	♐	♑	♒	♓	♈	♉	♊	♋	♌	♍	♎
DATE	*1st*	*3rd*	*6th*	*8th*	*10th*	*12th*	*14th*	*17th*	*19th*	*22nd*	*24th*	*27th*	*29th*	*31st*
TIME	*20.15*	*23.31*	*2.29*	*5.34*	*9.16*	*14.25*	*22.04*	*8.42*	*21.22*	*9.35*	*18.55*	*0.38*	*3.39*	*5.34*

'Moon phase' time slots last about 14 days. During each, the Moon passes through 6 or 7 zodiac divisions. Every other division ....

....constitutes a 'Zodiac' time slot, lasting 2 or 3 days, so there are roughly 3 whole or part 'Zodiac' slots within every 'phase' slot.

* *'Root veg.' group for Moon planting; 'All others' group applies to all other crops listed.*
] *Marks the end of the viable sowing time for listed crops in the location concerned, though some varieties may continue in other locations.*

1. Full & New Moons				January		REFER TO KEY ON PAGE 2.	

1. Full & New Moons

FULL DATE	NEW DATE	FULL DATE	NEW DATE
TIME	TIME	TIME	TIME

January

2. 'Moon phase' slots — REFER TO KEY ON PAGE 2.

* Root veg: 2 days before Full to 3 days before New.	FROM DATE	TO DATE	FROM DATE	TO DATE
All others: 2 days before New to 3 days before Full.	FROM DATE	TO DATE	FROM DATE	TO DATE

3. Slots when Moon is in Zodiacal signs: ♉ ♋ ♍ ♏ ♑ ♓ To complete, read key (page 2) & Sect. 3.(p.20)

SIGN	SIGN || SIGN	SIGN || SIGN	SIGN || SIGN	SIGN || SIGN	SIGN || SIGN	SIGN || SIGN	SIGN
DATE	DATE || DATE	DATE || DATE	DATE || DATE	DATE || DATE	DATE || DATE	DATE || DATE	DATE
TIME	TIME || TIME	TIME || TIME	TIME || TIME	TIME || TIME	TIME || TIME	TIME || TIME	TIME

First half of month

Outdoors - in open ground

Beans, broad
Spinach

Greenhouse & cold frame

Beans, broad

Heated frame & greenhouse

Beans, broad
Cabbages, early
*Carrots
Leeks, early
Lettuces, open
*Onions, Welsh
Peas

Plant out from g'house/frame

Rhubarb
*Shallots

Last half of month

Outdoors - in open ground

Beans, broad
Spinach

Heated frame & greenhouse

Aubergines
Beans, broad
Broccoli, Summer

Cabbages, early]
*Carrots
Cauliflowers, early
Kohl-rabi
Leeks, early]
Lettuces, open]
*Onions from seed
*Onions, Welsh
Peas
Peppers
Tomatoes

Greenhouse & cold frame

Beans, broad

Plant out from g'house/frame

Rhubarb
*Shallots

Some varieties may be sown earlier or later. Always check the seed suppliers' directions, & add your particular choices to the appropriate column.

Local climatic conditions, altitude & latitude also affect germination periods. Established local gardeners usually provide the best advice.

THE ANNUAL PLANTING LIST FOR ALL YEARS
A half-monthly sowing indicator; this may be used alone, or the
Moon planting time-slots applied. Sections 2 & 3 explain how.

Gwydion's Planting Guide

1. Full & New Moons				February			REFER TO KEY ON PAGE 2.			
FULL	NEW	FULL	NEW				2. 'Moon phase' slots			
DATE	DATE	DATE	DATE	*Root veg: 2 days before ⎱ FROM	TO		FROM	TO		
				Full to 3 days before New. ⎰ DATE	DATE		DATE	DATE		
TIME	TIME	TIME	TIME	All others: 2 days before ⎱ FROM	TO		FROM	TO		
				New to 3 days before Full. ⎰ DATE	DATE		DATE	DATE		

3. Slots when Moon is in Zodiacal signs: ♉ ♋ ♍ ♏ ♑ ♓ To complete, read key (page 2) & Sect. 3.(p.20)

SIGN	SIGN	SIGN	SIGN	SIGN	SIGN	SIGN	SIGN	SIGN	SIGN	SIGN	SIGN	SIGN	SIGN
DATE	DATE	DATE	DATE	DATE	DATE	DATE	DATE	DATE	DATE	DATE	DATE	DATE	DATE
TIME	TIME	TIME	TIME	TIME	TIME	TIME	TIME	TIME	TIME	TIME	TIME	TIME	TIME

First half of month

Outdoors - in open ground

Beans, broad
*Parsnips
Peas
Spinach

Greenhouse & cold frame

Beans, broad
Lettuces, open
*Turnips, Spring

Heated frame & greenhouse

Aubergines
Beans, broad
Broccoli, Summer
Cauliflowers, early
Kohl-rabi
Melons
*Onions from seed]
*Onions, Welsh
Peas

Plant out from g'house/frame

*Garlic
Rhubarb
*Shallots

Peppers
Tomatoes

Last half of month

Outdoors - in open ground

Beans, broad
*Parsnips
Peas

Greenhouse & cold frame

Beans, broad]
*Beetroot
Leeks, maincrop
Lettuces, open

Spinach

*Onions from seed
*Parsnips
Peas
*Radishes, black
*Turnips, Spring

Heated frame & greenhouse

Aubergines
Beans, broad]
Broccoli, Summer
Cauliflowers, early
Endive
Kohl-rabi
Melons
*Onions, Welsh
Peas
Peppers

Plant out from g'house/frame

*Garlic
Lettuces, open
*Shallots

Tomatoes

'Moon phase' time slots last about 14 days.
During each, the Moon passes through 6 or 7
zodiac divisions. Every other division ....

Page 4

....constitutes a 'Zodiac' time slot, lasting 2 or 3
days, so there are roughly 3 whole or part
'zodiac' slots within every 'phase' slot.

Section One

* *'Root veg.' group for Moon planting; 'All others' group applies to all other crops listed.*
] *Marks the end of the viable sowing time for listed crops in the location concerned, though some varieties may continue in other locations.*

March

REFER TO KEY ON PAGE 2.

[1.] Full & New Moons

FULL	NEW	FULL	NEW
DATE	DATE	DATE	DATE
TIME	TIME	TIME	TIME

	FROM	TO
* Root veg: 2 days before Full to 3 days before New.	FROM DATE	TO DATE
All others: 2 days before New to 3 days before Full.	FROM DATE	TO DATE

[2.] 'Moon phase' slots

FROM	TO
FROM DATE	TO DATE
FROM DATE	TO DATE

[3.] Slots when Moon is in Zodiacal signs: ♉ ♋ ♍ ♏ ♑ ♓ To complete, read key (page 2) & Sect. 3. (p.20)

SIGN	SIGN	SIGN	SIGN	SIGN	SIGN	SIGN	SIGN	SIGN	SIGN	SIGN	SIGN	SIGN	SIGN
DATE	DATE	DATE	DATE	DATE	DATE	DATE	DATE	DATE	DATE	DATE	DATE	DATE	DATE
TIME	TIME	TIME	TIME	TIME	TIME	TIME	TIME	TIME	TIME	TIME	TIME	TIME	TIME

First half of month

Outdoors - in open ground

*Artichokes, Chinese
Artichokes, globe
Beans, broad
Corn salad
Cress, American
Cress, garden
Mustard
Orache
Peas
Spinach
Watercress

Heated frame & greenhouse

Aubergines
Broccoli, Summer
Cauliflowers, early]
*Celeriac
Endive]
Fennel, Florence
Kohl-rabi]
*Onions, Welsh]
Spinach, N. Zealand
Tomatoes

Plant out from g'house/frame

*Artichokes, Jeruslm.
*Garlic
Onions, tree
*Shallots

Greenhouse & cold frame

*Beetroot
Brussels sprouts
Cabbages, Summer
*Carrots, early
Leeks, maincrop
Lettuce, cabbage
Lettuce, iceberg
Lettuce, open
*Onions from seed]
*Onions, Welsh
*Parsnips
Purslane, Winter
*Radishes
*Radishes, black
*Turnips, Spring

Last half of month

Outdoors - in open ground

*Artichokes, Chines.]
Artichokes, globe
Beans, broad
Corn salad
Cress, American
Cress, garden
Leaf beet

Lettuce, cos
Mustard
*Onions from seed
*Onions, silverskin
Orache
*Parsley, Hamburg
Peas
Roka
*Skirret

Plant out from g'house/frame

Spinach
Watercress

*Artichokes, Jeruslm.
Cabbages, early
*Garlic
Leeks, early
Onions, tree]
*Shallots

Continues overleaf

*Some varieties may be sown earlier or later.
Always check the seed suppliers' directions, & add
your particular choices to the appropriate column.*

*Local climatic conditions, altitude & latitude
also affect germination periods. Established
local gardeners usually provide the best advice.*

THE ANNUAL PLANTING LIST FOR ALL YEARS
A half-monthly sowing indicator; this may be used alone, or the
Moon planting time-slots applied. Sections 2 & 3 explain how.

Gwydion's Planting Guide

March continued

Heated frame & greenhouse

Aubergines]
Beans, French
Beans, runner

Broccoli, Summer]
Cardoons]
*Celeriac]
Celery
Cucumbers
Fennel, Florence]
Melons
Peppers
*Potatoes
Spinach, N. Zealand]
Tomatoes]

Greenhouse & cold frame

*Beetroot
Broccoli, Summer
Brussels sprouts
Cabbages, Summer]
Cauliflower, Sumr.]
*Carrots, early
Kohl-rabi

Leeks, maincrop]
Lettuce, cabbage
Lettuce, iceberg
Lettuce, open]
*Onions, Welsh
*Parsnips
Peas]
Purslane, Winter]
*Radishes
*Radishes, black
*Turnips, Spring

1.	Full & New Moons			# April		REFER TO KEY ON PAGE 2.	
FULL DATE	**NEW DATE**	**FULL DATE**	**NEW DATE**			2. 'Moon phase' slots	
TIME	**TIME**	**TIME**	**TIME**	* Root veg: 2 days before ⎫ FROM / Full to 3 days before New. ⎭ DATE	TO DATE	FROM DATE	TO DATE
				All others: 2 days before ⎫ FROM / New to 3 days before Full. ⎭ DATE	TO DATE	FROM DATE	TO DATE

3. Slots when Moon is in Zodiacal signs: ♉ ♋ ♍ ♏ ♑ ♓ To complete, read key (page 2) & Sect. 3. (p.20)

SIGN	SIGN	SIGN	SIGN	SIGN	SIGN	SIGN	SIGN	SIGN	SIGN	SIGN	SIGN	SIGN	SIGN
DATE	DATE	DATE	DATE	DATE	DATE	DATE	DATE	DATE	DATE	DATE	DATE	DATE	DATE
TIME	TIME	TIME	TIME	TIME	TIME	TIME	TIME	TIME	TIME	TIME	TIME	TIME	TIME

Outdoors - in open ground

Artichokes, globe
Beans, broad]
*Beetroot
Brussels sprouts
Cabbages, Autumn
Corn salad
Cress, American
Cress, garden
Leaf beet
Leeks, late
Lettuces, open
Lettuces, cos
*Mooli
Mustard
*Onions from seed
*Onions, silverskin

*Onions, Welsh
Orache
*Parsley, Hamburg
*Parsnips
Peas
Purslane, Winter
*Radishes
*Radishes, black
Rocket
Roka
*Salsify
*Scorzonera
*Skirret
Spinach
*Turnips, Spring
Watercress

First half of month

Heated frame & greenhouse

Beans, French]
Beans, runner]
Celery
Cucumbers
Gherkins]
Melons
Okra
Peppers]
*Potatoes]
Sweetcorn]

Plant out from g'house/frame

*Artichokes, Jeruslm.
Beans, broad
Cabbages, early
Cauliflower, early
*Garlic]
Kohl-rabi
Leeks, early]
Lettuces, open
*Onions from seed
*Onion sets
*Onions, Welsh
Peas
Rhubarb]
*Shallots

'Moon phase' time slots last about 14 days.
During each, the Moon passes through 6 or 7
zodiac divisions. Every other division ....

....constitutes a 'Zodiac' time slot, lasting 2 or 3
days, so there are roughly 3 whole or part
'zodiac' slots within every 'phase' slot.

* *'Root veg.' group for Moon planting; 'All others' group applies to all other crops listed.*
] *Marks the end of the viable sowing time for listed crops in the location concerned, though some varieties may continue in other locations.*

Greenhouse & cold frame

Amaranth
*Beetroot]

Broccoli, Summer
Broccoli, Winter
Brussels sprouts]
*Carrots, early]
Cauliflower, Summr.
Kohl-rabi

Lettuces, cabbage
Lettuces, iceberg
*Onions, Welsh]
*Parsnips]
Purslane
*Radishes]

Spinach, N. Zealand
*Turnips, Spring]

Outdoors - in open ground

Artichokes, globe
*Beetroot
Brussels sprouts]
Cabbages, Autumn]
*Carrots, early
Corn salad]
Cress, American
Cress, garden
Leaf beet
Leeks, late]
Lettuces, cos
Lettuces, open
*Mooli
Mustard
*Onions from seed]
*Onions, silverskin]
*Onions, Welsh
Orache
*Parsley, Hamburg]
*Parsnips]
Peas]
Peas, asparagus
*Potatoes
Purslane, Winter]
*Radishes
*Radishes, black
Rocket
Roka
*Salsify
*Scorzonera
*Skirret]
Spinach
*Turnips, Spring]
Watercress

Last half of month

Greenhouse & cold frame

Amaranth]
Broccoli, Summer]
Broccoli, Winter]
Cauliflowers, Summr.
Kohl-rabi]
Lettuces, cabbage]
Lettuces, iceberg]
Purslane
Spinach, N. Zealand

Heated frame & greenhouse

Celery]
Courgettes]
Cucumbers]
Marrows]
Melons]
Okra]

Plant out from g'house/frame

*Artichokes, Jeruslm.]
Beans, broad]
Brussels sprouts
Cabbages, early]
Cauliflowers, early]
Kohl-rabi
Lettuces, open]
*Onions from seed]
*Onion sets]
*Onions, Welsh
*Potatoes]
*Shallots]

Watering, slugs, snails and catch-crops!

This is the busiest time of year for sowing and planting, and for taking care of vulnerable seedlings. There may be dry periods which endanger produce from now until the end of the Summer. Water as necessary, using compost or mulch on top of the soil where appropriate to help retain moisture. Lettuces seem particularly keen to engage in a race to 'bolt' (sprouting a tall flowering stem and developing a bitter flavour) if the soil is dry for a significant period of time. The other inevitable problem concerns those hidden armies of slugs and snails which emerge during rainy spells, especially overnight. Use the solutions given in the section on organic pest control (page 29), and be persistent; regular onslaughts eventually diminish their numbers to a tolerable level! Plan successive sowings according to your crop rotation system (Section 4, page 30), and when sowing 'catch crops' (planting between established rows as crops are harvested or as space allows) make use of the 'companion crops' information (Section 4, page 24) for the most appropriate placement.

Some varieties may be sown earlier or later.
Always check the seed suppliers' directions, & add
your particular choices to the appropriate column.

Local climatic conditions, altitude & latitude
also affect germination periods. Established
local gardeners usually provide the best advice.

THE ANNUAL PLANTING LIST FOR ALL YEARS
A half-monthly sowing indicator; this may be used alone, or the
Moon planting time-slots applied. Sections 2 & 3 explain how.

Gwydion's Planting Guide

1. **Full & New Moons**

FULL DATE	NEW DATE	FULL DATE	NEW DATE
TIME	TIME	TIME	TIME

May

2. **'Moon phase' slots**

* Root veg: 2 days before ⎫ Full to 3 days before New. ⎭	FROM DATE	TO DATE	FROM DATE	TO DATE
All others: 2 days before ⎫ New to 3 days before Full. ⎭	FROM DATE	TO DATE	FROM DATE	TO DATE

3. Slots when Moon is in Zodiacal signs: ♉ ♋ ♍ ♏ ♑ ♓ To complete, read key (page 2) & Sect. 3.(p.20)

SIGN	SIGN	SIGN	SIGN	SIGN	SIGN	SIGN	SIGN	SIGN	SIGN	SIGN	SIGN	SIGN	SIGN
DATE	DATE	DATE	DATE	DATE	DATE	DATE	DATE	DATE	DATE	DATE	DATE	DATE	DATE
TIME	TIME	TIME	TIME	TIME	TIME	TIME	TIME	TIME	TIME	TIME	TIME	TIME	TIME

First half of month

Outdoors - in open ground

Beans, French
Beans, runner
*Beetroot
Broccoli, Summer
Broccoli, Winter
*Capucine
*Carrots, early
*Carrots, maincrop]
Chicory, blanching
Cress, American
Cress, garden
Fennel, Florence
Kale
Kohl-rabi
Leaf beet

Lettuces, cabbage
Lettuces, cos
Lettuces, iceberg
Lettuces, open
*Mooli
Mustard
*Onions, Welsh
Orache
Peas, asparagus
*Potatoes]
Purslane
*Radishes
*Radishes, black
Rampion
Rocket
Roka
*Salsify

Plant out from g'house/frame

Brussels sprouts
Cucumbers]
Endive]
Kohl-rabi
Lettuces, open
*Onions, Welsh

*Scorzonera
Spinach
Watercress

Greenhouse & cold frame

Beans, soya
Cauliflower, Sumr.]
Purslane
Spinach, N. Zealand]

Heated frame & greenhouse

Last half of month

Outdoors - in open ground

Beans, French
Beans, Runner
*Beetroot
Broccoli, Summer]
Broccoli, Winter]
*Capucine
*Carrots, early
Cauliflowers, Aut'm

Chicory, blanching]
Chicory, red
Cress, American
Cress, garden
Fennel, Florence]
Gherkins
Kale
Kohl-rabi
Leaf beet
Lettuce, cabbage

Lettuce, cos
Lettuce, iceberg
Lettuce, open
*Mooli
Mustard
*Onions, Welsh
Orache
Peas, asparagus]
Purslane
Radicchio

*Radishes
*Radishes, black
Rampion
Rocket
Roka
*Salsify]
*Scorzonera]
Spinach
Spinach, N. Zealand
Watercress

'Moon phase' time slots last about 14 days.
During each, the Moon passes through 6 or 7
zodiac divisions. Every <u>other</u> division ....

....constitutes a 'Zodiac' time slot, lasting 2 or 3
days, so there are roughly 3 whole or part
'zodiac' slots within every 'phase' slot.

* *'Root veg.' group for Moon planting; 'All others' group applies to all other crops listed.*
] *Marks the end of the viable sowing time for listed crops in the location concerned, though some varieties may continue in other locations.*

Plant out from g'house/frame

Amaranth
Aubergines
Beans, French
Beans, runner
Broccoli, Summer
Brussels sprouts

Cabbages, Summer
Cardoons]
Cauliflower, Summer
*Celeriac
Courgettes
Fennel, Florence
Kohl-rabi
Marrows
Melons
*Onions, Welsh]

Peppers
Sweetcorn
Tomatoes]

Heated frame & greenhouse

Greenhouse & cold frame

Beans, soya]
Chickpeas]
Purslane]

---

1. Full & New Moons				**June**		REFER TO KEY ON PAGE 2.	
FULL	NEW	FULL	NEW			2. 'Moon phase' slots	
DATE	DATE	DATE	DATE	* Root veg: 2 days before Full to 3 days before New.	FROM DATE — TO DATE	FROM DATE	TO DATE
TIME	TIME	TIME	TIME	All others: 2 days before New to 3 days before Full.	FROM DATE — TO DATE	FROM DATE	TO DATE

3. Slots when Moon is in Zodiacal signs: ♉ ♋ ♍ ♏ ♑ ♓ To complete, read key (page 2) & Sect. 3.(p.20)

SIGN	SIGN	SIGN	SIGN	SIGN	SIGN	SIGN	SIGN	SIGN	SIGN	SIGN	SIGN	SIGN	SIGN
DATE	DATE	DATE	DATE	DATE	DATE	DATE	DATE	DATE	DATE	DATE	DATE	DATE	DATE
TIME	TIME	TIME	TIME	TIME	TIME	TIME	TIME	TIME	TIME	TIME	TIME	TIME	TIME

Outdoors - in open ground

First half of month

Beans, French
Beans, runner
Beans, soya]
*Beetroot
Cardoons]
*Carrots, early
Cauliflowers, Autmn.
Chicory, red
Cress, American
Cress, garden
Gherkins]
Kale
Kohl-rabi
Leaf beet
Lettuces, cabbage
Lettuces, cos

Lettuces, cos
Lettuces, iceberg
Lettuces, open
*Mooli
Mustard
Mustard, Chinese
*Onions, Welsh]
Orache
Purslane
Radicchio
*Radishes
*Radishes, black
Rampion]
Rocket
Roka
Spinach
Spinach, N. Zealand
*Turnips]
Watercress

Amaranth]
Aubergines]
Beans, French]
Beans, runner]
Broccoli, Summer
Broccoli, Winter
Brussels sprouts]
Cabbages, Autumn
Cabbages, Summer
Cauliflowers, Sumr.]
*Celeriac]
Chickpeas
Courgettes]
Fennel, Florence]

Plant out from g'house/frame

Kohl-rabi
Marrows]
Melons]
Peppers]
Sweetcorn]

Continues overleaf

Some varieties may be sown earlier or later.
Always check the seed suppliers' directions, & add
your particular choices to the appropriate column.

Local climatic conditions, altitude & latitude
also affect germination periods. Established
local gardeners usually provide the best advice.

THE ANNUAL PLANTING LIST FOR ALL YEARS
A half-monthly sowing indicator; this may be used alone, or the
Moon planting time-slots applied. Sections 2 & 3 explain how.

Gwydion's Planting Guide

June continued

Greenhouse & cold frame

Heated frame & greenhouse

Composting adds humus to soil, helps retain moisture and will, in time, correct many deficiencies - a top layer now will help during hot Summer weather.

Outdoors - in open ground

Last half of month

Plant out from g'house/frame

Outdoors - in open ground	Last half of month		Plant out from g'house/frame
	Lettuces, cabbage	Spinach, N. Zealand	
	Lettuces, cos	Purslane	
Cauliflowers, Wintr.]	Lettuces, iceberg	Watercress]	Broccoli, Summer]
Beans, French	Lettuces, open		Broccoli, Winter]
Beans, Runner	*Mooli		Cabbages, Autumn]
*Beetroot	Mustard		Celery]
*Carrots, early]	Mustard, Chinese		Chickpeas
Chicory, green	Orache		Kohl-rabi
Chicory, red	Purslane]	**Heated frame & greenhouse**	
Cress, garden	Radicchio		
Cress, American	*Radishes		**Greenhouse & cold frame**
Endive	*Radishes, black		
Fennel, Florence	Rocket]		
Kohl-rabi	Roka		
Leaf beet	Spinach		

1. Full & New Moons				July				REFER TO KEY ON PAGE 2.	
FULL	NEW	FULL	NEW					2. 'Moon phase' slots	
DATE	DATE	DATE	DATE	* Root veg: 2 days before ⎫FROM		TO		FROM	TO
				Full to 3 days before New. ⎭DATE		DATE		DATE	DATE
TIME	TIME	TIME	TIME	All others: 2 days before ⎫FROM		TO		FROM	TO
				New to 3 days before Full. ⎭DATE		DATE		DATE	DATE

3. Slots when Moon is in Zodiacal signs: ♉ ♋ ♍ ♏ ♑ ♓ To complete, read key (page 2) & Sect. 3. (p.20)

SIGN	SIGN	SIGN	SIGN	SIGN	SIGN	SIGN	SIGN	SIGN	SIGN	SIGN	SIGN	SIGN	SIGN
DATE	DATE	DATE	DATE	DATE	DATE	DATE	DATE	DATE	DATE	DATE	DATE	DATE	DATE
TIME	TIME	TIME	TIME	TIME	TIME	TIME	TIME	TIME	TIME	TIME	TIME	TIME	TIME

Plant out from g'house/frame

First half of month

Chickpeas]   Kohl-rabi

'Moon phase' time slots last about 14 days.
During each, the Moon passes through 6 or 7
zodiac divisions. Every other division ....

Page 10

....constitutes a 'Zodiac' time slot, lasting 2 or 3
days, so there are roughly 3 whole or part
'zodiac' slots within every 'phase' slot.

* 'Root veg.' group for Moon planting; 'All others' group applies to all other crops listed.
] Marks the end of the viable sowing time for listed crops in the location concerned,
though some varieties may continue in other locations.

Outdoors - in open ground	Fennel, Florence] Kohl-rabi Leaf beet Lettuces, cabbage Lettuces, cos] Lettuces, iceberg Lettuces, open *Mooli Mustard Mustard, Chinese Orache Purslane Radicchio *Radishes	*Radishes, black Roka Spinach Spinach, N. Zealand *Turnips, Aut./Spring	Greenhouse & cold frame
Beans, French Beans, Runner *Beetroot Cabbages, pak choi Cauliflowers, Autm.] Chicory, green] Chicory, red Cress, American Cress, garden Endive]			Heated frame & greenhouse

Last half of month

Outdoors - in open ground	Lettuces, iceberg] Lettuces, open Mustard Mustard, Chinese *Mooli Orach] Purslane] Radicchio] *Radishes *Radishes, black Roka Spinach	Spinach, N. Zealand] *Turnips, Aut./Spring	Greenhouse & cold frame
Beans, French] Beans, runner] *Beetroot] Cabbage, pak choi Chicory, red Cress, American Cress, garden Kohl-rabi] Leaf beet Lettuces, cabbage		**Plant out from g'house/frame** Cauliflowers, Aut.] Kohl-rabi	Heated frame & greenhouse

1. Full & New Moons				August			REFER TO KEY ON PAGE 2.

FULL	NEW	FULL	NEW	* Root veg: 2 days before \ FROM	TO	FROM	TO
DATE	DATE	DATE	DATE	Full to 3 days before New. / DATE	DATE	DATE	DATE
TIME	TIME	TIME	TIME	All others: 2 days before \ FROM New to 3 days before Full. / DATE	TO DATE	FROM DATE	TO DATE

2. 'Moon phase' slots

3. Slots when Moon is in Zodiacal signs: ♉ ♋ ♍ ♏ ♑ ♓ To complete, read key (page 2) & Sect. 3.(p.20)

SIGN	SIGN	SIGN	SIGN	SIGN	SIGN	SIGN	SIGN	SIGN	SIGN	SIGN	SIGN	SIGN	SIGN
DATE	DATE	DATE	DATE	DATE	DATE	DATE	DATE	DATE	DATE	DATE	DATE	DATE	DATE
TIME	TIME	TIME	TIME	TIME	TIME	TIME	TIME	TIME	TIME	TIME	TIME	TIME	TIME

First half of month - continues overleaf

Some varieties may be sown earlier or later.
Always check the seed suppliers' directions, & add
your particular choices to the appropriate column.

Local climatic conditions, altitude & latitude
also affect germination periods. Established
local gardeners usually provide the best advice.

THE ANNUAL PLANTING LIST FOR ALL YEARS
A half-monthly sowing indicator; this may be used alone, or the
Moon planting time-slots applied. Sections 2 & 3 explain how.

Gwydion's Planting Guide

August continued

Outdoors - in open ground

Cabbages, pak choi
Cabbages, Winter
Cress, American
Cress, garden
Leaf beet
Lettuces, cabbage

First half of month

Lettuces, open
*Mooli
Mustard
Mustard, Chinese
*Radishes
*Radishes, black
Roka]
Spinach
*Turnips, Aut./Spr.

Greenhouse & cold frame

Cabbages, Spring
*Carrots, forcing
*Onions, Jap., Wintr.]

Plant out from g'house/frame

Kohl-rabi

Heated frame & greenhouse

Outdoors - in open ground

Cabbages, Winter]
Chicory, red
Corn salad
Cress, American]
Cress, garden]
Leaf beet
Lettuces, cabbage]

Last half of month

Lettuces, open]
*Mooli]
Mustard, Chinese]
*Onions, Jap., Wintr.]
*Radishes
*Radishes, black]
Spinach]
*Turnips, Aut./Spr.]
Winter Purslane]

Greenhouse & cold frame

Cabbages, Spring
*Carrots, forcing

Plant out from g'house/frame

Kohl-rabi]

Heated frame & greenhouse

September

1. Full & New Moons			
FULL DATE	NEW DATE	FULL DATE	NEW DATE
TIME	TIME	TIME	TIME

REFER TO KEY ON PAGE 2.

2. 'Moon phase' slots			
* Root veg: 2 days before Full to 3 days before New.	FROM DATE	TO DATE	
All others: 2 days before New to 3 days before Full.	FROM DATE	TO DATE	
	FROM DATE	TO DATE	
	FROM DATE	TO DATE	

3. Slots when Moon is in Zodiacal signs: ♉ ♋ ♍ ♏ ♑ ♓ To complete, read key (page 2) & Sect. 3.(p.20)

SIGN	SIGN	SIGN	SIGN	SIGN	SIGN	SIGN	SIGN	SIGN	SIGN	SIGN	SIGN	SIGN	SIGN
DATE	DATE	DATE	DATE	DATE	DATE	DATE	DATE	DATE	DATE	DATE	DATE	DATE	DATE
TIME	TIME	TIME	TIME	TIME	TIME	TIME	TIME	TIME	TIME	TIME	TIME	TIME	TIME

Outdoors - in open ground

First half of month

Cabbages, Spring
Chicory, red]

Corn salad
Leaf beet]

Lettuces, Winter
*Radishes]

*'Moon phase' time slots last about 14 days.
During each, the Moon passes through 6 or 7
zodiac divisions. Every other division ....*

*....constitutes a 'Zodiac' time slot, lasting 2 or 3
days, so there are roughly 3 whole or part
'zodiac' slots within every 'phase' slot.*

Section One

* 'Root veg.' group for Moon planting; 'All others' group applies to all other crops listed.
] Marks the end of the viable sowing time for listed crops in the location concerned, though some varieties may continue in other locations.

Greenhouse & cold frame

Cabbages, Spring
*Carrots, forcing
Lettuces, Winter

Heated frame & greenhouse

Broccoli, Spring
Cauliflowers, Spring
Endives

Plant out from g'house/frame

Outdoors - in open ground

Cabbages, Spring
Corn salad]
Lettuces, Winter

Last half of month

Heated frame & greenhouse

Broccoli, Spring]
Cauliflowers, Spr.]
Endives]

Greenhouse & cold frame

Cabbages, Spring
*Carrots, forcing
Cauliflowers, Spring]
Corn salad
Lettuces, Winter
*Radishes

Plant out from g'house/frame

1.	Full & New Moons			# October			REFER TO KEY ON PAGE 2.	
FULL	NEW	FULL	NEW				2. 'Moon phase' slots	
DATE	DATE	DATE	DATE	* Root veg: 2 days before Full to 3 days before New.	FROM DATE	TO DATE	FROM DATE	TO DATE
TIME	TIME	TIME	TIME	All others: 2 days before New to 3 days before Full.	FROM DATE	TO DATE	FROM DATE	TO DATE

3. Slots when Moon is in Zodiacal signs: ♉ ♋ ♍ ♏ ♑ ♓ To complete, read key (page 2) & Sect. 3. (p.20)

SIGN	SIGN	SIGN	SIGN	SIGN	SIGN	SIGN	SIGN	SIGN	SIGN	SIGN	SIGN	SIGN	SIGN
DATE	DATE	DATE	DATE	DATE	DATE	DATE	DATE	DATE	DATE	DATE	DATE	DATE	DATE
TIME	TIME	TIME	TIME	TIME	TIME	TIME	TIME	TIME	TIME	TIME	TIME	TIME	TIME

Outdoors - in open ground

Cabbages, Spring]
Lettuces, Winter]

First half of month

Greenhouse & cold frame

*Carrots, forcing
Lettuces, Winter]
*Radishes]
Spinach

Heated frame & greenhouse

Brussels sprouts
Cabbages, Spring]
Cauliflowers, Spr.

Plant out from g'house/frame

Continues overleaf

Some varieties may be sown earlier or later.
Always check the seed suppliers' directions, & add your particular choices to the appropriate column.

Page 13

Local climatic conditions, altitude & latitude also affect germination periods. Established local gardeners usually provide the best advice.

THE ANNUAL PLANTING LIST FOR ALL YEARS
A half-monthly sowing indicator; this may be used alone, or the
Moon planting time-slots applied. Sections 2 & 3 explain how.

Gwydion's Planting Guide

Hothouse crops grown during the Winter months

If using heated glasshouse facilities to grow exotic species or out-of-season crops during the Winter, the procedure remains exactly as given - stick to the monthly Moon-planting time-slots for sowing, planting and transplanting. There is still a noticeable improvement when Moon-planting in such unseasonally maintained environments, and this seems to hold true even when artificial lighting is used. The general opinion is that more subtle responses in plant development are at play, but no sound research is available. I suspect there are a few individuals with relevant experience, but gardening is more enjoyable to do than to write about!

October continued	Last half of month		Plant out from g'house/frame
Outdoors - in open ground	Greenhouse & cold frame	Heated frame & greenhouse	
	*Carrots, forcing] Spinach	Brussels sprouts] Cauliflowers, Spr.] Lettuces, Winter	

November

REFER TO KEY ON PAGE 2.

1. Full & New Moons					2. 'Moon phase' slots	
FULL DATE	NEW DATE	FULL DATE	NEW DATE	* Root veg: 2 days before ⎫ FROM DATE Full to 3 days before New. ⎭	TO DATE	FROM DATE TO DATE
TIME	TIME	TIME	TIME	All others: 2 days before ⎫ FROM DATE New to 3 days before Full. ⎭	TO DATE	FROM DATE TO DATE

3. Slots when Moon is in Zodiacal signs: ♉ ♋ ♍ ♏ ♑ ♓ To complete, read key (page 2) & Sect. 3. (p.20)

SIGN	SIGN	SIGN	SIGN	SIGN	SIGN	SIGN	SIGN	SIGN	SIGN	SIGN	SIGN	SIGN	SIGN
DATE	DATE	DATE	DATE	DATE	DATE	DATE	DATE	DATE	DATE	DATE	DATE	DATE	DATE
TIME	TIME	TIME	TIME	TIME	TIME	TIME	TIME	TIME	TIME	TIME	TIME	TIME	TIME

Outdoors - in open ground	First half of month		Plant out from g'house/frame
Beans, broad	Greenhouse & cold frame	Heated frame & greenhouse	
	Beans, broad Peas Spinach]	* Carrots, forcing Leeks Lettuces, Winter]	

'Moon phase' time slots last about 14 days.
During each, the Moon passes through 6 or 7
zodiac divisions. Every other division ....

Page **14**

....constitutes a 'Zodiac' time slot, lasting 2 or 3
days, so there are roughly 3 whole or part
'zodiac' slots within every 'phase' slot.

* *'Root veg.' group for Moon planting; 'All others' group applies to all other crops listed.*
] *Marks the end of the viable sowing time for listed crops in the location concerned, though some varieties may continue in other locations.*

Outdoors - in open ground	**Last half of month**		Plant out from g'house/frame
	Greenhouse & cold frame	Heated frame & greenhouse	
Beans, broad	Beans, broad Peas	* Carrots, forcing] Leeks]	

1. Full & New Moons				**December**		REFER TO KEY ON PAGE 2.	
FULL	NEW	FULL	NEW			2. 'Moon phase' slots	

FULL DATE	NEW DATE	FULL DATE	NEW DATE	* Root veg: 2 days before ⎫ FROM Full to 3 days before New.⎭ DATE	TO DATE	FROM DATE	TO DATE
TIME	TIME	TIME	TIME	All others: 2 days before ⎫ FROM New to 3 days before Full.⎭ DATE	TO DATE	FROM DATE	TO DATE

3. Slots when Moon is in Zodiacal signs: ♉ ♋ ♍ ♏ ♑ ♓ To complete, read key (page 2) & Sect. 3.(p.20)

SIGN	SIGN	SIGN	SIGN	SIGN	SIGN	SIGN	SIGN	SIGN	SIGN	SIGN	SIGN	SIGN	SIGN
DATE	DATE	DATE	DATE	DATE	DATE	DATE	DATE	DATE	DATE	DATE	DATE	DATE	DATE
TIME	TIME	TIME	TIME	TIME	TIME	TIME	TIME	TIME	TIME	TIME	TIME	TIME	TIME

Outdoors - in open ground	**First half of month**		Plant out from g'house/frame
	Greenhouse & cold frame	Heated frame & greenhouse	
Beans, broad	Beans, broad Peas		Broccoli, Spring Cabbages, Spring] Cauliflowers, Spring

Outdoors - in open ground	**Last half of month**		Plant out from g'house/frame
	Greenhouse & cold frame	Heated frame & greenhouse	
Beans, broad	Beans, broad Peas		Broccoli, Spring] Cauliflowers, Spr.]

Some varieties may be sown earlier or later.
Always check the seed suppliers' directions, & add
your particular choices to the appropriate column.

Local climatic conditions, altitude & latitude
also affect germination periods. Established
local gardeners usually provide the best advice.

THE PRIMARY TIMING TECHNIQUE
Germinating plants at the most advantageous times according to the
natural environmental cycles with which they (and we) evolved.

Gwydion's Planting Guide

WHY SOW ACCORDING TO LUNAR CYCLES?
AN AGE-OLD SKILL WITH A SOUND SCIENTIFIC BASIS
A brief explanation of some principles involved

All life on our planet has evolved with the cyclic nature of our natural environment. Night and day, the seasons, the intensity of light, and other factors have engendered our own sleep-patterns, metabolic cycles and so on. Plants also develop according to the cues provided by environmental cyclic changes.

The lunar cycles enable many advantageous adaptions; cut a beetroot or onion in half and you will see the growth rings or layers which grow with each lunar cycle. The vast tonnage of ocean tidal water shifted by the Sun and Moon's gravity each day illustrates just one such factor utilized by plants. Their vascular systems use capillary and 'valve' systems to convey sap, and these are particularly effective in utilizing gravitational variation (and atmospheric pressure, etc.) to assist capillary action.

Approaching a New Moon, as the Sun and Moon's gravity increasingly pull from the same direction, sap flow is assisted both upwards or downwards as the Earth revolves daily. Conversely, approaching a Full Moon the Sun and Moon's gravity pull from increasingly opposed directions and 'even out' this gravitational effect.

Full Moons bring a cycle of increasing light through the night hours, followed by a decrease until the dark period of a New Moon. Though not as intense as daylight, moonlight significantly assists photosynthesis and consequent growth characteristics throughout the cycle. Obviously, there are a host of other adaptions similarly affected.

Germination timing alters the delicate balance of potential development and growth. Some seeds will 'wait' for favourable times once germination is enabled by sowing. By understanding the Moon's effects, and timing sowing, planting, & transplanting accordingly, we can adapt the earliest stages of growth to favour either root or 'above-ground' development; thus we categorise all crops in one of these two easily defineable groups for the purposes of Moon planting, though there are other, more subtle effects as the Moon moves through each cycle.*

Modern superstition born of scientific 'reductionism' has caused this valuable knowledge to be much ignored in contemporary times. Perhaps the resurgence of 'organic' agriculture will re-establish this long-proven advantageous technique. Observation over thousands of years in many lands where agriculture is long-established, including Britain, has shown how the primary technique is best applied. To summarise in practical terms:

Germination enabled when the Moon waxes, i.e. when the Sun and Moon are in effect 'moving apart' will promote foliage, fruit or seed, in fact all 'above ground' development.
Germination enabled when the Moon wanes, i.e. when the Sun and Moon are in effect 'moving closer' will promote root development.

Periods from 2 days before the start to 3 days before the end of waxing or waning Moons are ideal, giving a 'flying start' to germination in either period.

---

* *Some of the more subtle effects of varying conditions caused by the lunar cycle are described in the introduction to Section 3.*

Page
16

Planting in the appropriate Moon phase seems particularly effective when applied to 'organically' grown produce.

Section Two

APPLYING THE TECHNIQUE
The 'Moon phase' time-slots begin two days before a New or Full Moon,
and end three days before the next Full or New Moon respectively.

THE PRIMARY TIMING TECHNIQUE
SOWING AND PLANTING WITH THE PHASES OF THE MOON

The waxing or waning Moon affects plant development in different ways. For the grower, thousands of years of experience lie behind this simple method of using the most advantageous periods within the natural lunar cycle. For this purpose, plants may be divided into 2 categories:

1. '**Root vegetables**' (indicated by an asterisk * in the Monthly Listings) in which root development is to be encouraged: Potatoes, carrots, beetroot, onions and so on.
   '**Root vegetables**' benefit if sowing, planting or transplanting is performed within 'time slots' from 2 days before a Full Moon to 3 days before the following New Moon.

2. '**All others**' literally - in which any growth above the soil is to be encouraged: leaf or salad vegetables, beans, peas or seeds, grains, fruit, cucurbits, and so on.
   These benefit from sowing, planting or transplanting performed within 'time slots' from 2 days before a New Moon to 3 days before the following Full Moon.

Look at the example below, extracted from the Key on page 2. Part 1. provides for Full and New Moon dates to be written in - please note there are spaces provided for the second Full or New Moon which will occur occasionally. Spaces are also provided for the exact time of day, though this is not essential.

Full and New Moon dates will enable you to enter the dates of the 'Moon Phase' slots in part 2. In this example, there is a New Moon on the 11th (at 23.10 hrs.), and a Full Moon on the 27th (at 13.23 hrs.).

1. Full & New Moons				**January**	REFER TO KEY ON PAGE 2.		
FULL	NEW	FULL	NEW		2. 'Moon phase' slots		
DATE	DATE *11th*	DATE *27th*	DATE	* Root veg: 2 days before) FROM *from* TO *8th* Full to 3 days before New.) DATE *start* DATE	FROM *25th* TO *to* DATE DATE *end*		
TIME	TIME *23.10*	TIME *13.23*	TIME	All others: 2 days before) FROM *9th* TO *24th* New to 3 days before Full.) DATE DATE	FROM TO DATE DATE		

From these entries, part 2. is easily completed, deducting 2 or 3 days from the Full and New dates as appropriate. After doing this, we can see that the month begins during a 'Root veg.' slot, which ends on the 8th (at 23.10 hrs, to be exact!) and an 'All others' slot starts on the 9th (also at 23.10 hrs. of course), ending on the 24th (13.23 hrs.) and the next 'Root veg.' slot starts exactly 24 hours later on the 25th (yes, at 13.23 hrs!) and continues after the end of the month.

Read this section again if necessary, and once you are sure you have understood the procedure, turn to the key on page 2. Note how the 'Moon phase' slots have been drawn in across the top of part 3., each spanning several of the shorter 'Moon in Zodiacal Sign' slots.

If you wish to use the further refinement of the 'Zodiac' time slots as given in Section 3, then complete that procedure before drawing in your 'Moon phase' slots to match the 'Zodiac' dates. Otherwise, you may draw in the 'Moon phase' slots anyway, illustrating the sequence of 'Root veg.' and 'All others' Moon Phase slots for quick reference.

If your diary or almanac does not give times for Full and New Moons, you may use the directions which follow to estimate, with sufficient accuracy, the current stage of the Moon's cycle.

When the 'Moon phase' time slots are written in
the monthly headings of Section 1, you will see
at a glance when to sow either plant category.

Page
17

The easiest way is to send for the Year Sheet
which provides each year's monthly headings,
already completed. See page 32 for details.

THE PRIMARY TIMING TECHNIQUE
Germinating plants at the most advantageous times according to the
natural environmental cycles with which they (and we) evolved.

Gwydion's Planting Guide

IDENTIFYING THE MOON PHASE
This fascinating technique is well worth learning -
you will always be able to predict Moonlit nights.

The Moon completes an orbit of the Earth roughly every 28 days. At New (also known as 'Dark') Moon, it is positioned most nearly in the direction of the Sun, so the unlit side faces the Earth. At Full Moon, its orbit has taken it to the other extreme, so we see the whole illuminated side of the Moon's surface. In order to determine the current stage of this cycle, simply observe the Moon, (whenever visible!) and note:

1. The time of day or night.
2. The approximate height of the Moon above the horizon - no need for measurement - just whether, for example, it is near the Eastern or Western horizon, or a third or maybe halfway towards the highest point it reaches. (Its 'zenith', which will be in the Southern sky.)
3. The portion of the Moon's face which is illuminated.

With the following information, your observation will enable a good estimate of the Moon's current position, so you may deduce the last and next New or Full Moon.

At New Moon, the Sun and Moon rise close together in the East and you won't see the Moon, because the side facing the Earth is in shadow and the Sun's light is so strong.
Each day, the Moon rises about an hour later, and 2 or 3 days after the New (Dark) Moon you may first spot the slim crescent of the 'New' phase descending in the Western sky towards sunset, following the Sun to the horizon.
As the waxing Moon sets an hour later each day, it becomes more visible until half its face is illuminated; this point is the 'First Quarter' (of the Moon's orbit.) You will recognize this stage because the Moon is at its highest position in the sky ('zenith') in the early evening, setting around midnight.
When Full Moon is reached 7 or 8 days later, the fully illuminated Moon will be rising in early evening, reaching its zenith at midnight, setting around dawn.
About 7 days later, the 'Last Quarter' is reached, with the half-illuminated Moon at its zenith in the early morning, at about dawn, setting around midday.
During the 'Last quarter' phase, The thinning crescent Moon will continue to be seen in the morning, until becomes too faint to see until after the 'Dark' New Moon.

Now try it yourself, following these illustrated examples.

Read each example, jot down your estimate, *then* compare with the conclusion given in each case.

After completing the examples, note how the crescent waxing/waning Moons roughly orientate as 'close brackets'/'open brackets' respectively.

Page **18**

These three examples of the Moon's appearance show the illuminated portion at different times during the cycle as seen from British latitudes.

Section Two

APPLYING THE TECHNIQUE
The 'Moon phase' time-slots begin two days before a New or Full Moon,
and end three days before the next Full or New Moon respectively.

DIRECTIONS

Read each example observation, and referring to the previous page, jot down the 3 points stated; the time, the approximate elevation & direction, and the portion illuminated. From these, you will be able to make your estimate, then check using the _'Conclusion'_ given after the example.

1. **You observe a crescent Moon fairly high in the South-Western sky, almost half illuminated, at about three hours after Sunset.**
Conclusion: As slightly less than half is illuminated, it must be either a day or two before 'First Quarter', or after 'Last quarter'.
As it is high in the Western half of the sky it must be setting, following the Sun to the horizon and perhaps five or six hours later. Therefore, it must be the Waxing Moon, one or two days before the First Quarter. It follows that the Full Moon will be about eight or nine days hence. (And obviously, an 'All others' planting slot period currently applies!)

2. **You observe a clear, almost completely illuminated Moon with just an edge indiscernable, low in the Western sky two hours after dawn.**
Conclusion: It must be within two or three days of Full Moon. It must be setting as it's in the West, so as the Sun has already risen, it follows that the Moon must be past Full. (Before Full Moon, it would have set before Sunrise.) Therefore, it must be two or three days after Full Moon. (It must also be a few days since the start of a 'Root veg.' Moon phase slot.)

3. **You observe an exactly half illuminated Moon, low in the Eastern sky, an hour before Midnight.**
Conclusion: The half-illuminated Moon can only be within a day or two of the First or Last Quarter. It must be just risen, being in the Eastern sky, and the Sun will rise roughly when the Moon is at its Zenith - it must be close to the 'Last Quarter'. (Which indicates the middle of a 'Root veg' Moon phase slot.)

Now go outside, look at the Moon and do it all by yourself! This method ensures you will always be able to estimate the Moon phase, not just for gardening, and know which nights will be most or least dark. Naturally, your estimate will not be absolutely precise, so allow a 'margin' of two days when applying it to the Moon phase slots herein, to be sure of sowing etc. within the appropriate time slot.* You will also find it intrigues those unfamiliar - and you'll receive requests to show how it's done! Use this Guide if verbal explanation proves complex - once properly learnt, the concepts are straightforward.

The easiest way of all is to send for:

GWYDION'S PLANTING GUIDE YEAR SHEET
(Available for every year, published the preceding June.)

This provides the twelve Monthly Headings from Section 1, already clearly completed, to be tucked into your Planting Guide for easy reference; this Planting Guide can thus be used for every year. Year Sheets cost £1.50p, (at the time of publishing, but just £1 for 1994) & a stamped, self-addressed envelope. Full details on page 32.

---

* _To allow these 2 day 'margins' shorten the Moon_
phase time slots by 2 days at each end. Start
'Root veg.' slots on Full Moon and end them ....

Page
19

....5 days before New Moon, and start 'All others'
time slots on New Moon, ending them 5 days
before Full Moon. See the Key on page 2.

THE SECONDARY TIMING TECHNIQUE
An introduction to the Moon's passage through the Zodiac, which   *Gwydion's Planting Guide*
has predictable but not completely explicable effects on plants.

DEFINING THE MOON'S ZODIACAL TIME-SLOTS
INTRODUCTION - A BRIEF OUTLINE OF THE FACTS AND THE ENIGMAS

There are twelve divisions (Signs) in the Zodiac, which may be regarded as 'fixed' divisions of the encircling 'globe' of space as seen from Earth. In sequence they are:

♈ ARIES, ♉ TAURUS, ♊ GEMINI, ♋ CANCER, ♌ LEO, ♍ VIRGO, ♎ LIBRA, ♏ SCORPIO, ♐ SAGITTARIUS, ♑ CAPRICORN, ♒ AQUARIUS, ♓ PISCES.

As the Moon completes a cycle roughly every 28 days, its orbit takes it through slightly more than 12 divisions, due to the Earth's own circular path as it orbits the Sun and other factors. Since ancient times observers have noted that when the Moon is 'in' every **alternate** Zodiacal Sign, sowing and planting produces consistently better overall results than during the intervening Signs. **The beneficial Signs for sowing, planting and similar activities are:**

♉ TAURUS, ♋ CANCER, ♍ VIRGO, ♏ SCORPIO, ♑ CAPRICORN, ♓ PISCES.

(Of astrological interest, these are alternately 'Earth' and 'Water' Signs; while the Moon is in 'Fire' and 'Air' Signs, plant propagation has been observed to produce comparatively unfavourable results.)

Therefore, by noting the times when the Moon 'enters' each Sign, the 'beneficial' Signs may be marked as 'Zodiacal' time-slots. To illustrate this for the Monthly Headings given in Section One, directions follow this introduction.

What causes variations in plant growth as the Moon traverses the Zodiacal divisions? The direct gravitational effect on us of distant stars is minute. Even a nearby planet such as Mars affects us less than someone walking across Australia! However, the surrounding cosmos, recent discoveries suggest, may cause changes at a very fundamental level. Every second, billions of sub-atomic particles and energies of various wavelengths pass through us from our Sun and more distant sources, their directions and characteristics moulded by the gravitational and other effects of the surrounding cosmos.

All life on our planet has evolved with this phenomena, and continues to do so. The comparatively recent discoveries of such continual bombardment perhaps go some way to explaining the much earlier observations of plant husbandry over many centuries. Perhaps this universal 'rain' of energy from elsewhere in the cosmos, its effect modified by the rhythm of our solar and lunar orbits has some effect on living matter. We are aware that the atomic structures of matter are subject to change in some ways due to these energies, but whether this causes variations in plant growth and other phenomena which we can define with the Zodiacal divisions remains unproven.

Speculation aside, the Chaldeans (circa 1000-500 b.c.e.) and others certainly knew of these effects, and enshrined them in legends and cultural knowledge. Twelve distinct divisions of the encircling skies, originally named after legendary constellations provide a convenient means of measurement. These divisions constitute the Zodiac, whose nomenclature is still used at the cutting edge of modern discovery; whether navigating by sextant or satellite-signal, computing the trajectory of a spacecraft or mapping a newly-discovered quasar, we still 'set our clocks' for Universal Time when the Sun 'enters' the first point of Aries. (The moment of the Spring or Vernal Equinox.)

The Zodiacal divisions resulted from the
observations of ancient peoples of cyclic events,
including plant growth, which coincided with....

Page
20

....astronomical cycles. Understanding the facts
dispels the mistaken assumption that anything
to do with astrology is superstition.

Section Three

APPLYING THE TECHNIQUE
Shorter 'Zodiac' time-slots are the best potential sowing times
within either of the longer 'Moon phase' time-slots.

DIRECTIONS - PLANNING ZODIACAL TIME-SLOTS FOR EACH MONTH

To do this, you will require a table of the Zodiac entry times for the Moon. This may be found in an astrological or astronomical ephemeris for the relevant year (not in all, check before buying) or certainly from the other sources detailed on page 32.

The example below is extracted from the key on page 2. Because each alternate Zodiacal Sign is beneficial for our purposes, the entries are paired together in boxes. By ensuring each box starts with a beneficial Sign, the first entry time in each box will be the start of a Zodiacal time-slot, the second entry time being the end of the slot. This is straightforward to achieve, as shown in the example below; look at part 3. .

On copying in the Moon Sign entry times, note whether the Moon is in a 'beneficial' sign at the start of the month. If so, copy that sign into the first space. If not, copy the first beneficial Sign, ignoring the initial unsuitable Sign. From there, simply copy in the entry dates/times in sequence, and each boxed pair of Signs will form the dates/times of the duration of each Zodiacal time-slot.

1. Full & New Moons				**January**		2. 'Moon phase' slots
FULL DATE	NEW DATE *11th*	FULL DATE	NEW DATE *27th*	* Root veg: 2 days before) FROM *from* TO DATE *start* DATE	8th	REFER TO KEY ON PAGE 2. FROM 25th TO *to* DATE *end*
TIME	TIME *23.10*	TIME *13.23*	TIME	Full to 3 days before New.)		
				All others: 2 days before) FROM 9th TO 24th		FROM TO DATE DATE
				New to 3 days before Full.) DATE DATE		

3. Slots when Moon is in Zodiacal signs: ♉ ♋ ♍ ♏ ♑ ♓ To complete, read key (page 2) & Sect. 3.(p.20)

← *Root veg.* — 8th/23.10 ↴ ↲ 9th — *All others* — 24th/13.23 ↴ ↲ 25th — *Root veg.* →

SIGN ♍	SIGN ♎	SIGN ♏	SIGN ♐	SIGN ♑	SIGN ♒	SIGN ♓	SIGN ♈	SIGN ♉	SIGN ♊	SIGN ♋	SIGN ♌	SIGN ♍	SIGN ♎
DATE *1st*	DATE *3rd*	DATE *6th*	DATE *8th*	DATE *10th*	DATE *12th*	DATE *14th*	DATE *17th*	DATE *19th*	DATE *22nd*	DATE *24th*	DATE *27th*	DATE *29th*	DATE *31st*
TIME *20.15*	TIME *23.31*	TIME *2.29*	TIME *5.34*	TIME *9.16*	TIME *14.25*	TIME *22.04*	TIME *8.42*	TIME *21.22*	TIME *9.35*	TIME *18.55*	TIME *0.38*	TIME *3.39*	TIME *5.34*

A typical Moon/Zodiac table

☽ Ingress	Date	Time	☽ Ingress	Date	Time
♍	1	20.15	♈	17	8.42
♎	3	23.31	♉	19	21.22
♏	6	2.29	♊	22	9.35
♐	8	5.34	♋	24	18.55
♑	10	9.16	♌	27	0.38
♒	12	14.25	♍	29	3.39
♓	14	22.04	♎	31	5.34

The table shows the Moon entering Virgo at 20.15 hrs. g.m.t. on the 1st day of the month. It must previously have been in Leo. Virgo is the first beneficial Sign, and thus forms the start of the first Zodiacal slot; 20.15 hrs. on the 1st, ending when the Moon enters Libra at 23.31 hrs. on the 3rd. The next slot begins when the Moon enters Scorpio and so on. Sufficient spaces are provided; simply ignore any initial slot of just a few hours duration (impractical for gardening!) and start with the first beneficial Sign after that.

When you complete this procedure with each Monthly Heading, you may show where the Moon phase time-slots overlie the newly-constructed Zodiacal time-slots, as in this example. In this way, the most advantageous times can be easily read with the month's sowing listings.

The easiest way is to send for the Year Sheet which provides each year's monthly headings, already completed. See page 32 for details.

MORE NATURAL TECHNIQUES A collection of popular
and specialist topics, with all the essential details,
in one Section for immediate reference.

Gwydion's Planting Guide

MOON PLANTING FOR ALL OTHER CROPS AND PLANTS

Directions for flowers, bulbs, fruit bushes and all trees, lawns and pasture, plough-in fallow mixtures, major cereal, food and other commercial crops, shrubs, hedges, imported exotic species and so on.

The essential principles described in Sections Two & Three apply to all species. Therefore, the majority will benefit from sowing, planting and transplanting during the seasonally appropriate 'All others' time-slots defined for Section One listed vegetables, as good 'above ground' development is usually the prime consideration.   Plants such as flowering bulbs fall within the 'All others' category, as enhanced flowering characteristics are important; enhancing either root or above ground development by lunar timing doesn't detract from the rest of the plant, it simply ensures the overall growth has characteristics best suited to the conditions at the time of either germination or the trauma of transplanting, and the Moon provides the necessary conditions.

Obviously, if root development is more important the 'Root veg.' time-slots apply, whether for food root crops and animal fodder roots such as beet, or specialist plough-in fallow or soil-fertilizing species where the matured roots are the effective soil nutrient source. Many roots such as beetroots, onions, and so on show their age by developing a growth ring each Moon's cycle as do slower and longer growing trees with each solar cycle; a good illustration of the effects of natural cyclic conditions on different species. No long-term research on the Moon-planting of trees has been published, so I recommend appropriate 'All others' time slots are adhered to; preferably with the Moon in a 'beneficial' Zodiacal Sign as previously discussed.

Time considerations for farmers and large-scale growers: When sowing and planting large-scale commercial crops, both 'primary' and 'secondary' Moon-planting time slots may prove impractical to follow as available time, imminent unsuitable weather and economics usually dictate the timetable. Generally, depending on the likely number of sowing/planting days needed, it should be possible to timetable within appropriate 14-day Moon phase time slots, which should give better overall results, and hopefully, within the 3-day beneficial Zodiac slots for the bulk of sowing. Obviously, it is not worth strictly adhering to these if the improved yield is at the risk of losing the whole crop by unseasonally delayed germination.

All life depends upon the rhythms of nature

| Fire Signs | Aries Leo Sagittarius | Earth Signs | Taurus Virgo Capricorn | **Page** **22** | Air Signs | Gemini Libra Aquarius | Water Signs | Cancer Scorpio Pisces |

Section Four

Moon planting for all other crops and plants: p. 22. Companion and incompatible crops: p. 24. Organic remedies for pests & diseases: p. 26. Crop rotation & composting: p. 30. Time adjustments for Daylight Saving Time: endpage.

AN ASTROLOGICAL MISCELLANY - COMMENTS AND TRADITIONS

It is a mistake to assume that the characteristics of an astrological natal chart apply to plants in the same way that an astrologer may define personality characteristics and predict events for a human subject. Whilst there is overwhelming evidence concerning specific subtle changes in human characteristics and affairs which are synchronously linked with configurations of planets, plants respond to their environment in specific growth & response patterns, the Sun and Moon being direct causal influences. They are tied to the annual cycles of the Sun in their growth pattern, and shorter-lived plants are generally more affected by lunar variations within each year. Planetary cycles are of different time-periods which preclude cyclic adaptions by plants. Similarly, it is impractical to attempt to use most planetary cycles for 'planet-planting', unless you wish to wait many years for a perfect configuration!

Some research exists wherein the effects of planets in particular Zodiacal Signs are recorded, but on close investigation such sample crops cannot compared with a simultaneous 'control group' sample, and results are judged very subjectively. Given a reasonable knowledge of what various astrological definitions actually define, and the obvious differences between plant and human organisms, to apply astrological techniques in this way is fundamentally inappropriate, though thorough research with correctly adapted astrological techniques is needed.

Given a reasonable knowledge of astrology, many readers will also realize that the astrological 'Houses' are also of little relevance to plant germination for similar reasons. Once again the scarcity of valid research is not surprising, partly because of the impracticality of perfect time-slots combining Moon, Zodiac, Planet and House configurations, and partly because the time-frames of astrological Houses are virtually irrelevant to the cyclic responses of plants. Moon planting is in effect the astrological framework appropriate to plant life in the same way that conventional astrology and interpretation applies to ourselves - and valid research exists which verifies beyond doubt certain aspects of both.

The following operations are traditionally performed during the periods stated.
Some are based on sound principles, others are more speculative - try them as convenient and note your results for future reference.

Sowing and planting: Rapidly growing climbing and trailing plants - sow/plant with the waxing Moon in an Air Sign. For tender leaves and mellow fruit - only with the waxing Moon in Water signs.

Harvesting: For juicy vegetables and fruit - immediately after Full Moon. Cereals: During a waxing Moon in Aries, Leo, or Aquarius. 'Hot' flavoured crops (horseradish, mustard, etc.): Harvest with the Moon in a Fire Sign.

Weeding: Only with the Moon in Virgo.

Composting and manuring: Only with the Moon in Scorpio between Last Quarter and New Moon. (Better plan well ahead if you're particularly pedantic!)

Pruning: For thicker growth - just after a New Moon, for less growth - after a Full Moon, this is also said to apply to haircuts. Chop firewood during a waning Moon, a 'drier' time.

Spraying: (Especially for organic gardening practices) - Moon in Virgo or Scorpio.

MORE NATURAL TECHNIQUES   *A collection of popular and specialist topics, with all the essential details, in one Section for immediate reference.*

Gwydion's Planting Guide

COMPANION & INCOMPATIBLE CROPS

Plan your 'INITIAL' crop from the list below, & 'ACCOMPANYING' crops from the list at the top.

How may crops of different species planted adjacently affect each other?

Because they absorb nutrients from the soil in different quantities which leaves some starved of essential substances, they deposit various waste products which affect others beneficially or detrimentally, and they produce specific chemical 'messages' intended to attract pollenating insects, repel predators or affect the growth characteristics of mutually beneficial or detrimental plant neighbours. Plants are very active in altering their immediate environment to their needs, so it is clearly worthwhile planting adjacent crops which benefit both, or at least the initial crop. The necessity for crop rotation (page 30) illustrates how successive crops of one type may leave soil impoverished.

The processes concerned are complex. Look at the accompanying table. An 'initial' crop (the vertical list) of Florence fennel will suffer if beans are planted with them, and looking at beans as an 'initial' crop, fennel will affect them detrimentally; they are mutually incompatible, but beans may be grown as a follow-on crop when the fennel is harvested. Some combinations will only affect one of the crops beneficially or detrimentally, other combinations will improve one crop and inhibit the other; for these reasons the accompanying table lists 'initial' crops as against 'accompanying' crops -

Initial \ Accompanying	ASPARAGUS	BEANS	BEETROOT	BRASSICAS	CARROTS	CELERIAC	CELERY	CHERVIL	CHICORY	CORN SALAD
ASPARAGUS										
BEANS			C	C	C	C	C			
BEETROOT	X	C		X						
BRASSICAS		C	C				C			
CARROTS		C	X	C			C		C	
CELERIAC		C		C	C					
CHICORY					C					
CUCURBITS	C	C	C	C			C			
ENDIVE		C		C	C			C		
FENNEL, FLOR.	X								C	C
GARLIC	X	X	C	X	C	C			C	
KOHL RABI	C	C	C	C			C			
LEAF BEET					C					
LEEKS						C	C		C	
LETTUCES	C	C	C	C						
ONIONS	X	X	C	X	C	C			C	
PARSNIPS		C	C	C	C					
PEAS				C		C				
POTATOES		C	X	C			X			
RADISHES		C		C	C			C		
SALSIFY		C		C	C	C				
SCORZONERA		C		C	C	C				
SPINACH		C		C	C					
STRAWBERRIES		C			X	C				
SWEETCORN		C	X				X			
TOMATOES	C	C	C	C	C		C		C	
TURNIPS		C	C		C		C		C	

this ensures the 'initial' crop will always benefit, and 'accompanying' crops will usually benefit also when 'compatible' combinations are used. When sowing and planting combinations in this way, intersperse rows or individual plants with regard to the spacing and light which each requires. Note that some species (e.g. rhubarb, sage) only appear as 'accompanying' crops; it is unlikely they will be grown in interspersed crop between rows. suitable ways to allow a normally

Moon planting for all other crops and plants: p. 22. Companion and incompatible crops: p. 24. Organic remedies for pests & diseases: p. 26. Crop rotation & composting: p. 30. Time adjustments for Daylight Saving Time: endpage.

	CUCURBITS	DILL	ENDIVE	FENNEL, FL.	GARLIC	KOHL RABI	LEAF BEET	LEEKS	LETTUCES	ONIONS	PARSLEY	PARSNIPS	PEAS	POTATOES	RADISHES	RHUBARB	SAGE	SALSIFY	SCORZON'A	SPINACH	STRAWBER'S	SWEETCORN	TOMATOES	TURNIPS
ASPAR.	C				X	C		X	C	X													C	
BEANS	C	C	C	X	X	C		X	C	X			C	C	C						C	C	C	C
BEETS.	C	C			C			X	C	C			C	X						X	C	X		
BRASC.	C	C	C		X				C	X				C		C	C			C	X		C	
CARROT		C	C		C		▲	C	C	C	C		C		C			C	C	C	C		C	
CELERC.								C	C	C			C				C		C				C	
CHICRY.			C							C													C	
CUCRB.	■		C	C					C	C			C	X	X				▲			C	X	
ENDIVE	C		■	C	X	C			C	C	X		C				C						C	
FENNEL	C		C	■					C				C	▲			C						X	
GARLIC	C	C			■				C		C	C	X	X				C	C		C		C	C
KOHL R.	▲		▲	▲		■			C				C	C	C			C	C	C				▲
LEAF B.							■							C										
LEEKS		C						■	C	C			X					C	C		C		C	
LETTUC.									■															
ONIONS	C	C						C		■	C	C	X	X				C	C		C		C	C
PARSNIP										C			C								C			
PEAS	C	C	C	C	X	C		X	C	X			■	C								C	X	C
POTATO		X		▲	C									■				C		C			C	C
RADISH	X				C	C	C	C	C	C			C		■			C	C				C	
SALSIFY			C		C			C	C									■		C				
SCORZ.			C		C			C	C										■	C				
SPINCH.					C								C	C	C					■		C	C	
STRAW.	X			C				C	C	C	C			C						C	■			
SWEETC.	C	C							C				C	C								■	C	
TOMATO	X			X	C			C	C	C	C		X		C					C		C	■	X
TURNIP								C	C				C	C						C			X	■

Legend

☐C☐ Compatible combination

☒ Incompatible combination

▲ After harvesting 'initial' crop, the 'accompanying' crop is seasonally convenient and a good follow-on.

This table contains only proven combinations - spaces indicate no effect or insufficient research, and many....

Page 25

....species have never been sufficiently recorded for compatibility, so experiment and note your results.

DISCLAIMER: *Due to current legislation, all home-made remedies on pages 26-29 are simply 'foliar applications', their specific uses being stated for historical interest only....*

Gwydion's Planting Guide

ORGANIC REMEDIES FOR PESTS AND DISEASES

To avoid traces of toxic substances in your soil and garden produce, organic controls are an advantage to any gardener, and generally very effective. Many disorders are easily identified, and their remedies are mostly simple to prepare or buy. To identify more obscure disorders you will need to refer to a detailed specialist text - there are hundreds of potential disorders well beyond the scope of this and other books, so if necessary contact one of the organizations given on the last page. However, you will be able to deal with many using the details herein including the description of methods for dealing with slugs & snails - an essential topic for all gardeners!

TWELVE TREATMENTS AND THEIR PREPARATION

When applying sprays or other 'watery' preparations, always add a little soft soap or a good squirt of biodegradable washing-up liquid, sufficient to break down the surface tension of the water and allow complete soaking of the affected foliage or predator with the active ingredients. Some remedies will specify more soap. If further applications of organic treatments are necessary, it is usually possible to use stronger concentrations without any danger to the crops concerned. By all means make up smaller or larger quantities of preparations as required, just keep the proportions of ingredients about the same; unlike 'chemical' gardeners, you will not be polluting your soil or exceeding critical concentrations. Don't throw away the plant residue after straining, let it drain thoroughly then add to the compost - but not a quantity which would concentrate too much of one species in your compost. When applying sprays, be sure to reach the underside of all foliage.

A. **Chamomile maceration spray** Soak fresh or dried chamomile flowers in water (around a couple of handfuls per pint) overnight, and strain, squashing the residue with the (gloved) hands to extract most of the active ingredients, then mix in a dash of washing-up liquid before spraying.

B. **Derris powder or spray** (Made from a Malayan fish-poison plant) Buy the natural rather than synthetic preparation and use as directed by the manufacturers. The natural version also breaks down quickly to avoid affecting the food chain.

C. **Horsetail infusion spray** Collect or buy horsetail (*equisetum arvense*) and boil the stems (they seem to be mainly stem!) for half an hour in water (5 or 6 oz. per pint) then cool and strain etc. as in A. above. Dilute in up to 100 times as much water, less for a stronger concentration, add a little soap, then spray.

D. **Methylated spirit application ('soap-spirit')** Mix about a quarter to half an ounce of methylated spirit and a similar quantity of soap or washing-up liquid into a quart of water, agitate to foam and apply the foam directly to the predator-infested parts. Repeat once or twice daily as required, and increase the concentration of methylated spirit if necessary - it's doubtful that you will damage the plant by the time the predators are dealt with.

E. **Nematodes (eelworms), Encarsia formosa (tiny wasps)** Several parasitic species are bred for organic control of specific predators by specialist suppliers. (See below)

F. **Nettle manure spray** Fill a bucket with loosely-packed nettle foliage, fill with cold

Specialist advice for obtaining parasitic species to kill several specific pests is available from the organizations listed....

Page **26**

....on the last page, and their advised publications may be borrowed through your local library's interlibrary loan service.

water and cover. After a week it will smell good & potent! Strain, etc. as in A., with the advantage that the nettles add good plant nutrients to the soil. N.B: Rhubarb leaves will act as a substitute in most cases; prepare in the same way, or use the stronger preparation, J. below, if necessary.

G. **Pyrethrum spray** Fresh or dried flowers of feverfew or various species of chysanthemum (particularly *chrysanthemum cinerarifolium*) are made up and used as in A. above. The naturally derived preparation may be bought; unlike the synthetic substitute it leaves the food-chain quickly, though it will kill some beneficial insects as well as predators whilst in use. Allow several days to disperse before harvesting.

H. **Quassia wood infusion spray** Buy quassia wood (*quassia cortex*) shavings and add 10 oz. to half a gallon of water. Soak for 24 hours, then boil for 1 hour. Cool, strain, dilute by up to 1 in 10, add the usual dash of washing-up liquid before spraying.

J. **Rhubarb infusion spray** Cut rhubarb leaves into small pieces and add to water (2 lbs. per half-gallon) then boil for 1 hour. Cool, strain etc. as in A.

K. **Tobacco maceration/infusion spray** Soak an ounce of tobacco (preferably pipe tobacco or similar; cigarettes contain too much saltpetre, etc.) in a gallon of water overnight, Strain, etc. as in A. above. An infusion made by boiling is stronger, but smells awful in the kitchen! Dispose of the tobacco residue, don't put it in the compost.

L. **Sulphur preparation** Buy a proprietory brand and use as directed by manufacturers.

M. **Copper/copper sulphate preparation** Buy and use as directed by manufacturers.

DIRECT ACTIONS

1. Remove and burn or similarly destroy the affected tips or parts. Be sure to remove all necessary material; use any of the advised treatments as well if the problem persists.
2. Keep seeds cool; buy the vulnerable species of seed in sealed packets and keep cool after opening; also wrap opened seed pack in suitable cloth to prevent predator entry.
3. Use insect netting over the crop, be careful not to enclose predators as well!
4. Remove and burn or similarly destroy all the affected crop. (Or remaining affected seeds as appropriate.)
5. Remove predators or despatch them 'in situ' by hand.
6. Intersperse african marigolds amongst crop.

---

68 COMMON PESTS & DISEASES
The disorders are listed overleaf with appropriate treatments (A. to M.) direct actions to take (1. to 6.) and other advice.

You will probably be familiar with the most common ailments and it's always worth trying a likely cure with those you don't recognise, and refer to a specialist book on plant diseases and pests if necessary - then select the treatment and/or action listed. Make sure sprays and similar treatments reach the underside of leaves.

Where several options are given choose one or more, and for some ailments two or more necessary treatments and actions are indicated. E.g. American gooseberry mildew: both C. *and* 1. are necessary, Aphids: D. F. G. and J. are possible options to choose from.

---

68 COMMON DISORDERS

American gooseberry mildew: C. and 1.

Aphids: D. F. G. J.

Asparagus beetles: B. and plant nasturtiums between asparagus rows.

Bean beetles (in bean seeds): 4., 2.

Bean seed flies: K. on soil, next time 3. and don't sow directly after brassicas, lettuces or spinach.

Bean and pea weevil: G

Beet flies: (leaf miner, mangold fly): 1. and try D. or K. and 3. for unaffected rows; difficult without 'chemical' treatment.

Big bug mites: Black currants especially: as soon as flower clusters visible D. or F., treat regularly thereafter.

Blackfly: Treat as aphids

Blight: (rust, leafspot): C.

Cauliflower 'blindness' (no heart): Growing tip damaged; ensure smooth transition and watering when planting out.

Botrytis (grey mould): C. L.

Cabbage blackrot: More space between plants, don't over-promote foliage development.

Cabbage Moths: 3. and G.

Cabbage root flies: Place 8" square 'collars' of carpet/underlay closely around stem at ground level, and F.

Cabbage thrips: Try B. and 3.

Cane spot: (spur blight): M. in April, again after picking.

Carrot flies: 4. (non-eatable plants and infected parts), 3. and intersperse with Spring onions, spread wood-ash. Also 3., with fine carrot fly netting.

Caterpillars (generally): 5. and/or G.

Cauliflower 'flowering': Avoid excess water & nitrogen, use resistant varieties.

Chafer beetles: Trap under placed balls of wood shavings, 3., try G.

Chocolate spot: No cure. 1., and grow resistant varieties, use good seed.

Club root: No cure; plant in 'bottomless pots', avoid brassicas in infected location for several years, ensure soil pH = 7.

Codling moths: Trap on greased and sticky bands secured around trunk.

Colorado beetle: Don't disturb & inform Ministry of Ag. immediately - legal requirement.

Cutworms: Dig out from around plants, 5., try G. and K. on soil.

Damping off: Sow on fresh seed compost, covering seeds with silver sand.

Downy mildew: A., try C., use resistant varieties. No onions in affected plot for several years.

Earwigs: Traps: Damp straw in flowerpots upside down.

Eelworms: 4, 5 and treat soil....

....& wash roots with K. or D. & transplant elsewhere, don't put vulnerable crops there: 6 years at least, 9 years for potatoes.

Flea beetles: K., lime, wood-ash. Trap with sugar-syrup.

Green capsid bugs: G.

Greenfly: As aphids.

Grey mould: See Botrytis.

Halo blight: No cure. 1. and use good seed, crop rotation.

Leaf blotch (fungus types): C. L.

Leaf hoppers: C. L.

Leaf rollers: B.

Leaf spot: C.

Leatherjackets: G.

Leek moths: G. and 3.

Mealy aphids: Difficult. Try D. and 1.

Onion flies: F. and 3. and 6.

Pea weevil: See bean weevil

Pea moths: Spray: infusion of african marigold, garlic & onion leaves, and 6.

Pea thrips: G. when flower-buds apparent.

Potato blight: C. L.

Potato scab: Soil too limey. Add lots of compost.

Powdery mildew: C. L.

Raspberry beetles: B.

Redberry mites: L. when fruiting shoots reach 6", again just before flowering.

Red spider mite: D. or F. and keep plants damp.

Rings in lettuces: Shelter from cold winds.

Section Four

....It is illegal to use them or advise their use because they cannot be precisely quantified or regulated. Please use expensive toxic sprays instead, as preferred by inflexible bureaucrats who would be better employed turning over your manure heap.

Root aphids: Move roots from infected plot, rinsing with K.

Root eelworms As root aphids, and 5.

Rust: See Blight.

Sawflies: B.

Scab: (on beetroot): No cure. Try more compost.

Scale insects: D. and 5.

Sclerotinia (barkrot): Wider spacing, don't sow directly after chicory, cucurbits, endives, lettuce, avoid all these in location for several years.

Slugs, snails: Accompanying text gives most solutions.

Springtails: D. K.

Spur blight: See cane spot.

Strawberry mites: D. or F. and 3.

Strawberry seed beetles: Try B. or D. and 3.

Thrips: B.

Vine weevils: Difficult. Drown in water for several hours if possible, try G. repeatedly, or E. (nematodes)

Viruses (generally): No real cure; use resistant varieties. Symptoms often confused with nutrient deficiencies.

Whiptail: Insufficient molybdenum in soil, try less composting & proprietory foliar fertilizer spray.

Whitefly: Tricky. Intersperse french marigold, Try B. and G. or E. (encarsia formosa)

White rot: See Sclerotinia.

Wireworms: 5 and G. B.

SLUGS & SNAILS
The most popular garden pests!

Conventional chemical slug pellets containing metaldehyde and similar treatments are grossly irresponsible - birds and hedgehogs die after eating the dying molluscs and the pellets themselves - and both assist you by feeding on these and other pests. There are three better methods: trapping, barriers, and safer selective poisons. With perseverance, their numbers can be reduced to a manageable level.

Trapping They will shelter under wooden planks laid on the ground and may be collected daily for disposal - this method and barriers will appeal to those wishing to transport them elsewhere rather than kill them. Also, hunt them with a torch when they feed after dark; you will hear them moving and munching on quiet evenings. Use only shallow saucers containing milk/water mix as drowning traps; steep-sided traps indiscriminately kill small creatures including mammals and useful insects, as does the much-used beer/sugar mixture, which also attracts and poisons hedgehogs. Milk will help attract pest-eating hedgehogs, and a good compost heap may become home to equally useful slow-worms.

Barriers Eggshells crushed to drawing-pin head size and splintery sawdust make reasonable barriers, but need renewing regularly. Plastic lawn-edging and similar little 'walls' (4" above ground level will suffice) are ideal to stop slugs & snails as they can't cross the sharp edge.

Acceptable poisons Aluminium sulphate, sold under brand names such as 'fertosan' will not kill birds and hedgehogs, and used sparingly will not add unacceptable levels of aluminium to soil or the water-table. It can be applied as powder (on soil, not foliage unless it's lightly raining or about to) or dissolved and watered onto soil to kill slugs burrowing for shelter. Follow the suppliers' directions. The other very effective acceptable poison is easy to make; mix one part of alum to seven parts of slaked lime and sprinkle thinly on the soil. Most simply, a thin sprinkling of ordinary salt will despatch them, then rain or watering will disperse it.

All these methods will do the trick, and regular treatments or removal over time will reduce the slug & snail population in the immediate locality quite noticeably, and weeding and well-trimmed grass will deny them cover.

African marigolds amongst vegetable plots keep several pests at bay, as do spring onions amongst most root crops.

Bindweed and couch grass: remove, dig out the white roots and don't place in the compost - every scrap will regenerate.

MORE NATURAL TECHNIQUES *A collection of popular and specialist topics, with all the essential details, in one Section for immediate reference.*

Gwydion's Planting Guide

CROP ROTATION SYSTEMS TO SUIT YOUR GARDEN

Growing the same crop in a patch of soil year after year will exhaust the nutrients and minerals the species uses most and may form a suffocating surplus of its waste products which can be useful to other species. Similarly, diseases specific to the species will proliferate and the nutrient imbalance will cause various disorders. Since early times, areas of the Earth have been turned to desert by this means; the Romans and Egyptians of classical times, some Celtic peoples and Native Americans have all learnt about crop rotation the hard way. More recently, the Great Dust Bowl in the U.S.A. is the result of attempting continuous grain production. Using chemical fertilizers continually will ruin the soil eventually; nature will set the limits.

The more years you can include in a rotation cycle the better; it depends on the area you have available and the crops you wish to grow. You need a minimum of a 3-year cycle to keep a plot healthy; if you can manage six nominal plots you may gain the most benefit with a 6-year cycle. Below are plans for 3 to 6 year cycles; select one to suit your garden or allotment, and if you have just one small plot, cycle it through a 3 or 4 year rotation. For any rotation of less than 6 years, give brassicas a miss in any particular plot for several years now and then to avoid club root and onions to avoid downy mildew, etc.

For planning rotation, vegetables are divided into groups to grow in each plot in turn.

3-YEAR ROTATION

GROUP 1.
(Crops producing nitrogen)
Legumes: Peas and beans; any type or combination.

GROUP 2.
(Crops requiring nitrogen)
Potatoes, leaf vegetables, brassicas (cabbage family), cucurbits (cucumber family: marrows, courgettes, etc.) celeriac, leeks, tomatoes.

GROUP 3.
Other root vegetables: Beets, carrots, fennel, onions, parsnips, etc.

YEAR 1.
Plot 1: Group 1.
Plot 2: Group 2.
Plot 3: Group 3.

YEAR 2.
Plot 1: Group 2.
Plot 2: Group 3.
Plot 3: Group 1.

YEAR 3.
Plot 1: Group 3.
Plot 2: Group 1.
Plot 3: Group 2.

4 to 6-YEAR ROTATION

GROUP 1.
(Crops producing nitrogen)
Legumes: Peas and beans; any type or combination. As each is harvested, plant brassicas for overwintering.

GROUP 2.
(Crops requiring nitrogen)
More brassicas; Spring crop was planted the previous year. As Spring crops are lifted, plant outdoor tomatoes. As later brassicas are harvested, plant other leaf vegetables: lettuces, etc., also radishes, swedes, turnips.

GROUP 3.
Other root vegetables: Beets, carrots, fennel, kohlrabi, onions, parsnips, salsify....

....also leaf vegetables: lettuces, etc., in rows not used for leaf vegetables the previous year.

GROUP 4.
(Crops producing nitrogen again)
Legumes: Peas and beans; any type or combination, and strawberries if convenient. As legumes are harvested, leave fallow adding compost, comfrey and other enriching manures.

GROUP 5.
Potatoes; As early crop is harvested, plant leeks. As maincrop is harvested, plant broad beans, with later sowings for overwintering.

FALLOW YEAR.
Feed soil with compost, green manure, etc., and/or plant fallow mixture including comfrey and dig in before seeding occurs.

For a tiny plot where rotation is difficult, grow vegetables which don't need rotation: Green salad vegetables, leaf beet....

Page 30

....radishes, spring onions, some carrots now & then, etc. Swap rows as possible, compost well. Tomatoes, etc: grow in containers.

Section Four

Moon planting for all other crops and plants: p. 22. Companion and incompatible crops: p. 24. Organic remedies for pests & diseases: p. 26. Crop rotation & composting: p. 30. Time adjustments for Daylight Saving Time: endpage.

4-YEAR

YEAR 1.
Plot 1: Group 1.
Plot 2: Group 2.
Plot 3: Group 3.
Plot 4: Group 5.

YEAR 2.
Plot 1: Group 2.
Plot 2: Group 3.
Plot 3: Group 5.
Plot 4: Group 1.

YEAR 3.
Plot 1: Group 3.
Plot 2: Group 5.
Plot 3: Group 1.
Plot 4: Group 2.

YEAR 4.
Plot 1: Group 5.
Plot 2: Group 1.
Plot 3: Group 2.
Plot 4: Group 3.

5-YEAR

YEAR 1.
Plot 1: Group 1.
Plot 2: Group 2.
Plot 3: Fallow.
Plot 4: Group 3.
Plot 5: Group 5.

YEAR 2.
Plot 1: Group 2.
Plot 2: Fallow.
Plot 3: Group 3.
Plot 4: Group 5.
Plot 5: Group 1.

YEAR 3.
Plot 1: Fallow.
Plot 2: Group 3.
Plot 3: Group 5.
Plot 4: Group 1.
Plot 5: Group 2.

YEAR 4.
Plot 1: Group 3.
Plot 2: Group 5.
Plot 3: Group 1.
Plot 4: Group 2.
Plot 5: Fallow.

YEAR 5.
Plot 1: Group 5.
Plot 2: Group 1.
Plot 3: Group 2.
Plot 4: Fallow.
Plot 5: Group 3.

6-YEAR

YEAR 1.
Plot 1: Group 1.
Plot 2: Group 2.
Plot 3: Fallow.
Plot 4: Group 3.
Plot 5: Group 4.
Plot 6: Group 5.

YEAR 2.
Plot 1: Group 2.
Plot 2: Fallow.
Plot 3: Group 3.
Plot 4: Group 4.
Plot 5: Group 5.
Plot 6: Group 1.

YEAR 3.
Plot 1: Fallow.
Plot 2: Group 3.
Plot 3: Group 4.
Plot 4: Group 5.
Plot 5: Group 1.
Plot 6: Group 2.

YEAR 4.
Plot 1: Group 3.
Plot 2: Group 4.
Plot 3: Group 5.
Plot 4: Group 1.
Plot 5: Group 2.
Plot 6: Fallow.

YEAR 5.
Plot 1: Group 4.
Plot 2: Group 5.
Plot 3: Group 1.
Plot 4: Group 2.
Plot 5: Fallow.
Plot 6: Group 3.

YEAR 6.
Plot 1: Group 5.
Plot 2: Group 1.
Plot 3: Group 2.
Plot 4: Fallow.
Plot 5: Group 3.
Plot 6: Group 4.

> If your brassicas, onions or spuds suffer persistent disorders, grow only overwinter & Spring varieties for several years.

SOME BRIEF TIPS ON COMPOSTING

In making compost, the aim is to imitate natural humus in the soil as nearly as possible, avoiding transfer of persistent infections and weeds whose roots can survive composting. Use all your garden weedings and plant/lawn trimmings with these exceptions: Heavy or woody material which cannot be 'chipped', no material with the long-lived infections requiring burning etc., (pages 26-29) no brassica or tomato roots, no chemically treated material, no large quantities of dog's mercury, and absolutely no bindweed or couch grass. Use also your raw kitchen vegetable waste but no cooked or animal or dairy produce, and never the contents of the vacuum cleaner bag!

Make a proper compost container about 2' 10" square, as described in most general gardening books. Two such containers will produce a continual supply; fill one whilst using the other, a large garden may require several. An uncovered pile of garden waste will not do - rain washes nutrients away, and insufficient heat is generated.

What should I do with cooked kitchen leftovers?

The idea of a compost heap is to concentrate micro-organisms which specifically break down plant material, so kitchen waste will slow the process. Other micro-organisms and particular worms which naturally feed on such material are easy to employ in a worm-culture bin; kits, including live worms are commercially available, and produce excellent liquid and solid soil nutrients.

How can I enrich an impoverished or newly prepared vegetable plot?

Deciduous leafmould, and/or manure, fresh or well-rotted, are both good to 'start' a new plot. Leaves decompose largely by fungi - once again, it would slow down your compost heap, and as with fresh manure it is best heaped and covered separately. Either may be dug into the topsoil fresh by mid-Autumn for a first 'breakcrop' planting of potatoes or similar in the Spring.

Gwydion's Planting Guide

(Mail ordering details revised at Midsummer, 2003.
After 2005, please write for updated details, enclosing an s.a.e.)

You can buy tables of Moon/Zodiac entry times from various sources,
or send for our annual Year Sheets and other publications by mail order

Many bookshops and stationers stock Moon/Zodiac tables in annually published astrological almanacs for popular readership such as 'Raphaels', and some astrologers' annual 50 or 100 year Ephemeris Tables (from good bookshops) also state the Moon Zodiac entry times - not all though, so check before buying. The publishers of this Guide also sell two interesting little yearly publications which always give the necessary Moon times: Gwydion McPagan's Moon Calendar (A3 poster format) and Gwydion McPagan's Moon Diary. (Cream card cover, similar format to this Guide, A5 booklet.) These, and our Year Sheets are available for each year, from the preceding Summer/Autumn - see below for details.

Our annual Year Sheets make Moon planting easy!

The annual Year Sheets are published 6 months in advance, so from late June onwards, you may write for the next year's Year Sheet. It provides the monthly fill-in boxes as in Section One of this Guide, already completed for immediate Moon planting use. Year Sheets fold to the same dimensions as this Guide to tuck in as a convenient bookmark.

To buy one or more Year Sheets, write to the address below enclosing:

1. Your request stating clearly for which year you need one or more Year Sheets.
2. Payment of £1.50p per Year Sheet by cheque or postal order payable to: J. R. Gower.
3. A stamped, self-addressed envelope of A5 capacity, the size of this Guide when closed.
    (Our £1.25p postage and packaging fee does not apply to Year Sheets when
    you provide an s.a.e. See details below for some of our other publications.)

J. R. Gower (mail order),
11, Summerhouse Orchard Cottages,
Bove Town,
GLASTONBURY,
Somerset.
BA6 8JA

'Gwydion's Planting Guide' or our other publications can also be ordered by mail, enclose payment by cheque or postal order payable to: J. R. Gower.

Gwydion's Planting Guide, The Definitive Moon Planting Manual
One to nine copies: £4.99p per copy, add £1.25p postage & packaging fee to the total.
Ten or more copies: £3 per copy, no postage/packaging fee.

G. McP's Moon Diary: One to nine copies: £3.75p each, add £1.25p p&p to the total.
Ten or more copies: £2.25p each, no postage/packaging fee.

G. McP's Moon Calendar poster: One to nine copies: £2.50p each, add £1.25p p&p to the total. Ten or more copies: £1.35p each, no postage/packaging fee.

All postage & packaging prices herein apply within the U.K. only.
Overseas orders: Write with details of quantities required, enclosing a self-addressed envelope.

Gwydion's Planting Guide
The Definitive Moon Planting Manual
ISBN 0 9523424 0 5
© 1994, J. R. Gower.